Classic

TUSCAN

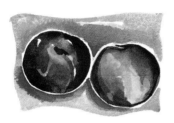

Classic
TUSCAN

ULTIMATE
EDITIONS

First published by Ultimate Editions in 1996

© 1996 Anness Publishing Limited

Ultimate Editions is an imprint of
Anness Publishing Limited
1 Boundary Row
London SE1 8HP

This edition distributed in Canada by Book Express
an imprint of Raincoast Books Distribution Limited

ISBN 1 86035 134 4

Publisher Joanna Lorenz
Senior Cookery Editor Linda Fraser
Designer Ian Sandom
Illustrations Madeleine David
Photographers Karl Adamson, Edward Allwright and Steve Baxter
Introduction Christine Ingram
Recipes Carla Capalbo
Food for photography Wendy Lee and Jane Stevenson
Stylists Blake Minton and Kirsty Rawlings
Jacket photography Thomas Odulate

Printed and bound in Singapore

For all recipes, quantities are given in both metric and imperial measures, and, where appropriate,
measures are also given in standard cups and spoons. Follow one set, but not a mixture,
because they are not interchangeable.

Pictures on frontispiece, page 7, 8 and 9: Zefa Pictures

CONTENTS

FOREWORD

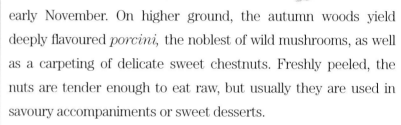

Tuscany is one of Italy's most varied regions, famous for the cypress-studded Chianti hills which run between Florence and Siena. It is bound to the north by the Apennine mountains and to the west by a long stretch of Mediterranean coastline.

Until recently, most Tuscans were country people who lived simply working the land and its produce. Their cooking was based purely on seasonal foods, both cultivated and wild, and made the best use of the resources of man and nature. It still does.

In spring, Tuscans of all ages scour the country fields, armed with thick gloves and plastic bags or baskets. They may be searching for early nettles, wild fennel or the bitter salad leaves

that they are so fond of. "Wild greens cleanse the blood," an old woman explained as she stooped to cut dandelion shoots with a small knife. "But always leave the roots undamaged, to safeguard next year's growth."

Summer brings an abundance of tender beans and vegetables. Combined with fresh herbs and even day-old crusty bread, they go into the making of the thick peasant soups, the staples of this healthy cuisine. In autumn, as the new season's Chianti is being harvested in the area's picturesque sloping vineyards, some of the dark aromatic grapes are baked into rustic breads like the *Schiacciata con Uva*, or they are eaten with local pheasant or quail, available after the hunting season starts in early November. On higher ground, the autumn woods yield deeply flavoured *porcini*, the noblest of wild mushrooms, as well as a carpeting of delicate sweet chestnuts. Freshly peeled, the nuts are tender enough to eat raw, but usually they are used in savoury accompaniments or sweet desserts.

From November to January, vast orange nets are stretched beneath the bushy grey-green trees as men and women hand-pick olives for the region's "liquid gold" – the extra virgin olive oil which is often still stone-ground and cold-pressed at a nearby *frantoio* or mill. It is this fruity green oil, with its peppery aftertaste, which colours so many of Tuscany's best dishes. Try them, using the freshest ingredients you can find, and you too will enjoy the inimitable taste of Tuscany.

CARLA CAPALBO

INTRODUCTION

There is a timelessness about Tuscany so pervasive that you feel that if this indeed were the Garden of Eden, then little has changed since the days of Adam and Eve. The landscape of lush green hills, studded with Cyprus trees and dotted with ancient churches and castles has, since Etruscan times, harnessed the imaginations of painters and poets, each in turn captivated by its grace and beauty.

In the fourteenth century, Florence became the major city of the region and under the patronage of the influential Medici family, the genius of Michelangelo, Da Vinci and other great artists, poets, writers and philosophers, made Tuscany the very centre of the Renaissance.

Equally as alluring is the cuisine of this romantic region: its secret is in its simplicity. Rich sauces and elaborate garnishes

play no part in the Tuscan repertoire. The Tuscans have always despised excess and favoured light and healthy dishes made with the freshest of local ingredients.

Guiseppe Prezzolini, a writer of the early twentieth century, described Tuscan cooking as "light, lean, tasty and full of character and

Lush green fields and sunflowers (right) and a traditional city market (above) are typically Tuscan, while fresh vegetables and herbs (left) are central to this simple cuisine.

fragrance, created for people of lively intellect who do not wish to sit around and grow fat". Even in the wealthiest of homes, you are likely to be served an unelaborate meal with a simple salad dressed with the finest olive oil.

Almost all Tuscan meals are served with bread. Unlike other parts of Italy, pasta and rice play only minor roles in Tuscan cuisine. *Brushetta al Pomodora* – a bread brushed with olive oil and garlic, then toasted and served with chopped tomatoes, is served in restaurants all over Tuscany, while at home, house-wives concoct a pungent and filling Tomato and Bread Soup that they often serve with *crostini* – rustic canapés, brushed with olive oil and toasted over a wood fire. *Crostini* can be served with a variety of toppings, but chopped chicken livers, seasoned with sage or spicy puréed beans are both favourites.

In other parts of Italy, Tuscans are often referred to as *Mangiafagioli* or "bean eaters" because of their penchant for dried beans, particularly cannellini and other haricot varieties. Tuscan Baked Beans, *Fagioli al Forno alla Toscana*, is a celebrated regional dish, enjoyed in homes and restaurants.

Vegetables, grown throughout the region, are used in starters, soups, with pasta or meat and served in an array of vegetarian dishes. Meats and fish are mainly grilled or roasted and vegetables are cooked simply and quickly. There are few rules, beyond the golden rule that food must be fresh.

The fine olive oil, for which Tuscany is deservedly famous, is widely used in cooking and for making simple dressings. There are many varieties, ranging in colour from pale gold to deep green – the strong, spicy varieties are mixed with lemon juice and vinegar to make simple salad dressings, while the milder-flavoured oils are used for everyday cooking.

Fresh herbs, particularly sage, rosemary and basil, are other popular Tuscan ingredients, as are, come autumn, chestnuts and mushrooms that are gathered from the woods and fields.

The lasting image of Tuscany is without a doubt the summer custom of people eating together. During the afternoon, long trestle tables are set under the vines or in the shade of olive trees and families and friends then gather together to enjoy the best of Tuscan fare and a bottle or two of Chianti.

WHITE BEAN SOUP

Minestrone di Fagioli

A thick purée of cooked dried beans is at the heart of this substantial country soup. It makes a warming winter lunch or supper dish.

INGREDIENTS

350g/12oz/1½ cups dried cannellini or other white beans
1 bay leaf
75ml/5 tbsp olive oil
1 onion, finely chopped
1 carrot, finely chopped
1 celery stick, finely chopped
3 tomatoes, peeled and finely chopped
2 garlic cloves, finely chopped
5ml/1 tsp fresh thyme leaves, or 2.5ml/½ tsp dried thyme
750ml/1¼ pints/3 cups boiling water
salt and ground black pepper
extra virgin olive oil, to serve

SERVES 6

1 Pick over the beans carefully, discarding any grit. Place them in a large bowl, add cold water and soak overnight. Drain the beans, tip them into a large saucepan, cover with water, and bring to the boil. Cook for 20 minutes. Drain. Return the beans to the clean pan, cover with cold water, and bring to the boil again. Add the bay leaf, and cook for 1–2 hours or until the beans are tender.

2 Drain the beans, discarding the bay leaf. Set aside a quarter of the beans and purée the rest in a food processor, or pass through a food mill, adding a little water to stop them sticking if necessary.

3 Heat the oil in a large saucepan. Add the onion. Cook, stirring for 5 minutes or until it softens. Add the carrot and celery, and cook for 5 minutes more.

4 Stir in the tomatoes, garlic and thyme, then cook for a further 6–8 minutes, stirring frequently.

5 Pour in the boiling water. Stir in the reserved beans and the bean purée. Season with salt and pepper. Bring to the boil, then simmer for 10–15 minutes. Serve in soup bowls, drizzled with a little olive oil.

TOMATO AND BREAD SOUP

Pappa al Pomodoro

This colourful Florentine recipe makes marvellous use of bread that has begun to go stale. Make it with very ripe fresh or canned tomatoes.

INGREDIENTS
90ml/6 tbsp olive oil
1 small piece dried red chilli,
crumbled (optional)
175g/6oz bread, cut into 2.5cm/1in cubes
1 onion, finely chopped
2 garlic cloves, finely chopped
675g/1½lb ripe tomatoes peeled and
chopped, or 2 x 400g/14oz cans peeled
plum tomatoes, chopped
45ml/3 tbsp shredded fresh basil
1.5 litres/2½ pints/6½ cups light
meat stock or water, or a mixture
salt and ground black pepper
extra virgin olive oil, to serve (optional)

SERVES 4

1 Heat 60ml/4 tbsp of the oil in a large saucepan. Add the chilli, if using, and stir for 1–2 minutes. Add the bread cubes and cook until golden. Using a slotted spoon, transfer them to a plate lined with kitchen paper, then leave to drain.

2 Add the remaining oil to the pan, add the onion and garlic and cook for 5 minutes. Add the tomatoes, bread cubes and basil. Season with salt. Cook over a medium heat, stirring occasionally, for 15 minutes.

3 Meanwhile, heat the stock or water in a separate pan. When it starts to simmer, pour it into the tomato mixture and stir well. Bring to the boil, lower the heat and simmer for 20 minutes.

4 Remove the pan from the heat. Use a fork to mash the tomatoes and the bread together. Season with pepper, and add more salt if necessary. Allow to stand for about 10 minutes. Just before serving, swirl in a little extra virgin olive oil, if you like.

PASTA AND LENTIL SOUP

Pasta e Lenticchie

The small brown lentils which are grown in central Italy are usually used for this wholesome soup, but green lentils may be substituted, if preferred.

INGREDIENTS

225g/8oz/1 cup dried green or brown lentils
90ml/6 tbsp olive oil
50g/2oz/¼ cup diced ham or salt pork
1 onion, finely chopped
1 celery stick, finely chopped
1 carrot, finely chopped
2 litres/3½ pints/8 cups chicken stock or water, or a mixture
1 fresh sage leaf or a pinch of dried sage
1 fresh thyme sprig or 1.5ml/¼ tsp dried thyme
175g/6oz/1½ cups ditalini or other small soup pasta
salt and ground black pepper

SERVES 4–6

1 Pick over the lentils carefully, discarding any small stones or other pieces of grit. Place them in a bowl, add cold water to cover, and soak for 2–3 hours.

2 Heat the oil in a large saucepan. Sauté the ham for 2–3 minutes. Add the onion, and cook for 5 minutes. Stir in the celery and carrot, and cook for 5 minutes more.

3 Drain the lentils, rinse them well, then drain again. Add them to the pan, stirring thoroughly to coat them in the fat. Pour in the stock or water, with the herbs, and bring the soup to the boil. Cook over a medium heat for about 1 hour or until the lentils are tender.

4 Stir in the pasta and cook until just tender. Season with salt and pepper to taste. Allow the soup to stand for a few minutes before serving in heated bowls.

RICE AND BROAD BEAN SOUP

Minestra di Riso e Fave

This thick soup makes the most of fresh broad beans while they are in season. It works well with frozen beans for the rest of the year.

INGREDIENTS

*1kg/2¼lb broad beans in their pods, or
400g/14oz shelled broad beans,
thawed if frozen
90ml/6 tbsp olive oil
1 onion, finely chopped
2 tomatoes, peeled and finely chopped
225g/8oz/1 cup risotto rice
25g/1oz/2 tbsp butter
1 litre/1¾ pints/4 cups boiling chicken
stock or water
salt and ground black pepper
freshly grated Parmesan cheese,
to serve (optional)*

SERVES 4

1 Shell the beans if they are fresh. Bring a large saucepan of water to the boil, add the fresh or frozen beans and blanch them for 3–4 minutes. Drain the beans, rinse under cold water, then drain again. Squeeze the beans between finger and thumb to pop them out of their skins.

2 Heat the oil in a large saucepan. Add the onion and cook over a low heat for 5 minutes until it softens. Stir in the beans, and cook for about 5 minutes, stirring often to coat them with the oil. Season with salt and pepper. Add the tomatoes and cook for 5 minutes more, stirring often.

3 Stir in the rice and cook for 1–2 minutes, then add the butter, stirring until it melts. Pour in the stock or water, a little at a time. Continue cooking the soup until the rice is tender. Taste for seasoning and adjust if necessary. Serve hot, with grated Parmesan, if using.

FISH SOUP

Ciuppin

his hearty soup makes a meal in itself, with toasted French bread or chunks of ciabatta.

INGREDIENTS

1kg/2¼lb mixed whole fish or fish fillets
(such as coley, dogfish, whiting, red
mullet or cod)
90ml/6 tbsp olive oil, plus extra to serve
1 onion, finely chopped
1 celery stick, chopped
1 carrot, chopped
60ml/4 tbsp chopped fresh parsley
175ml/6fl oz/¾ cup dry white wine
3 tomatoes, peeled and chopped
2 garlic cloves, finely chopped
1.5 litres/2½ pints/6 cups hot fish stock
or water
salt and ground black pepper
rounds of French bread, to serve

SERVES 6

1 Scale and clean any whole fish, discarding all innards, but leaving the heads on. Cut the fillets into large pieces. Rinse in cold water, and pat dry with kitchen paper. Heat the oil in a large pan and cook the onion over a low heat for 5 minutes. Stir in the celery and carrot, and cook for 5 minutes more. Add the parsley.

2 Pour in the wine, raise the heat, and cook until the liquid has reduced by half. Stir in the tomatoes and garlic. Cook for 3–4 minutes, stirring occasionally. Pour in the stock or water, and bring to the boil. Cook over a medium heat for 15 minutes.

3 Stir in the fish. Simmer for 10–15 minutes, or until it is tender. Season with salt and pepper. Remove the fish from the soup with a slotted spoon. Discard any skin or bones, then purée the flesh in a food processor or pass through a food mill.

4 Stir the fish purée into the saucepan, until well combined. Heat the soup to simmering point. Toast the bread, and drizzle lightly with olive oil. Place two or three pieces of bread in each heated soup bowl, then pour on the soup.

COOK'S TIP
If the soup is cooked until it reduces to the consistency of a sauce, it makes an excellent topping for pasta.

CROSTINI WITH MUSSELS OR CLAMS

Crostini con Cozze o Vongole

E ach of these seafood crostini is topped with a mussel or clam, and then baked. Use fresh seafood whenever possible for the best flavour.

INGREDIENTS
16 large mussels or clams, in their shells
250ml/8fl oz/1 cup water
4 large slices of bread, 2.5cm/1in thick
40g/1½oz/3 tbsp butter
1 shallot, very finely chopped
30ml/2 tbsp chopped fresh parsley
olive oil, for brushing
lemon quarters, to serve

MAKES 16

1 Preheat the oven to 190°C/375°F/Gas 5. Place the prepared mussels or clams in a saucepan, add the water and bring to the boil. Cover the pan, lower the heat and simmer the shellfish for 5–7 minutes until their shells open. Lift them out of the pan, remove them from their shells, and set aside. Discard any that remain closed.

2 Slice the crusts off the bread and cut into quarters. Taking care not to cut through to the bottom, scoop out a hollow large enough to hold a mussel or clam. Set the bread squares (crostini) aside.

3 Crumb the scooped-out bread in a food processor, or use a grater. Melt the butter in a frying pan. Cook the shallot, parsley and breadcrumbs over a low heat for 4 minutes, until the shallot softens.

4 Brush each crostini with olive oil. Place a mussel or clam in each hollow. Spoon a small amount of the parsley and shallot mixture on to each mussel or clam. Place on an oiled baking sheet and bake for about 10 minutes. Serve immediately, with the lemon quarters.

HARD-BOILED EGGS WITH TUNA SAUCE

Uova Sode Tonnate

T he simple combination of eggs with a tasty tuna mayonnaise makes a nourishing first course that is quick and easy to prepare.

INGREDIENTS
6 size 1 eggs
200g/7oz can tuna in olive oil
60ml/4 tbsp olive oil
3 drained canned anchovy fillets
15ml/1 tbsp drained capers
30ml/2 tbsp freshly squeezed lemon juice
salt and ground black pepper
capers and anchovy fillets, to garnish

FOR THE MAYONNAISE
1 egg yolk, at room temperature
5ml/1 tsp Dijon mustard
5ml/1 tsp white wine vinegar or lemon juice
150ml/¼ pint/⅔ cup olive oil

SERVES 6

1 Place the eggs in a saucepan of cold water. Bring to the boil and cook for 8–10 minutes. Drain, then cool in cold running water. Shell carefully and set aside.

2 Make the mayonnaise by whisking the egg yolk, mustard and vinegar or lemon juice in a bowl. Whisk in the oil a few drops at a time until about a third of it has been incorporated. Pour in the remaining oil in a slow stream, whisking constantly.

3 Place the tuna, with its oil, in a blender or food processor. With the motor running, gradually add the olive oil, to make a thick sauce. Add the anchovies, capers and lemon juice and process until smooth.

4 Stir the mixture into the bowl of mayonnaise, mix well and season with black pepper. Add salt if necessary. Cover and chill for at least 1 hour.

5 Cut the eggs in half lengthways. Arrange on a serving platter. Spoon on the sauce and garnish with capers and anchovy fillets. Serve chilled.

GRILLED FRESH SARDINES

Sarde alla Griglia

F resh sardines are flavourful and firm-fleshed, and quite different in taste and consistency from those canned in oil. They are excellent simply grilled and served with lemon.

INGREDIENTS
*1kg/2¼lb very fresh sardines, gutted and
with heads removed
olive oil, for brushing
45ml/3 tbsp chopped fresh parsley
salt and ground black pepper
lemon wedges, to garnish*

SERVES 4

1 Preheat the grill. Rinse the sardines in cold water. Pat dry with kitchen paper.

2 Brush the sardines lightly with olive oil and sprinkle generously with salt and pepper. Place in a single layer in a grill pan. Grill for 3–4 minutes.

3 Turn the sardines over and cook for 3–4 minutes more, or until the skin begins to brown. Sprinkle with the parsley and serve immediately, garnished with lemon wedges.

19

SPAGHETTI WITH GARLIC AND OIL

Spaghetti con Aglio e Olio

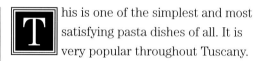

This is one of the simplest and most satisfying pasta dishes of all. It is very popular throughout Tuscany.

INGREDIENTS
400g/14oz spaghetti
90ml/6 tbsp extra virgin olive oil
3 garlic cloves, chopped
60ml/4 tbsp chopped fresh parsley
salt and ground black pepper
freshly grated Parmesan cheese,
to serve (optional)

SERVES 4

1 Cook the spaghetti in a large saucepan of rapidly boiling salted water for 12 minutes, or for the amount of time suggested on the packet.

2 Meanwhile, heat the oil in a large frying pan and gently sauté the garlic until it is barely golden. Do not let it brown or it will taste bitter. Stir in the chopped parsley. Season with salt and pepper, then remove the pan from the heat.

3 As soon as the pasta is *al dente*, tip it into the frying pan with the oil and garlic. Return the pan to the heat and cook for 2–3 minutes, tossing the spaghetti to coat it with the sauce. Serve at once in a warmed serving bowl, with Parmesan, if using.

TROUT BAKED IN PAPER WITH OLIVES
Trota in Cartoccio con Olive

aper parcels retain all the flavour of the fish and add an element of surprise to a dinner party.

INGREDIENTS

4 oven-ready trout, about 275g/10oz each
75ml/5 tbsp olive oil
4 bay leaves
4 slices pancetta
60ml/4 tbsp chopped shallots
60ml/4 tbsp chopped fresh parsley
120ml/4fl oz/½ cup dry white wine
24 green olives, stoned
salt and ground black pepper

SERVES 4

1 Preheat the oven to 200°C/400°F/Gas 6. Rinse the trout under cold running water. Pat dry with kitchen paper.

2 Cut four pieces of non-stick baking paper, each large enough to enclose one fish and brush with oil. Lay one fish on each piece of paper. Place a bay leaf in each cavity, and sprinkle with salt and pepper.

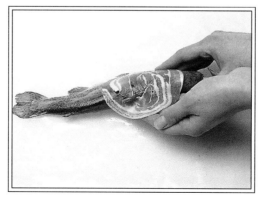

3 Wrap a pancetta slice around each fish, sprinkle with the shallots and parsley, then drizzle with the remaining oil and the white wine. Add 6 olives to each.

4 Close the paper loosely around each fish, rolling the edges together to seal them completely. Place on a baking sheet and bake for 20–25 minutes. Arrange each packet on a plate and open at the table.

BAKED AROMATIC SEA BASS

Branzino Aromatizzato al Forno

Sea bass is a firm white-fleshed fish which benefits from simple cooking. Use fresh herbs, if possible, for the tastiest dish.

INGREDIENTS
1 large sea bass, about 1.5kg/3–3½lb
4 bay leaves
few thyme sprigs
8–10 parsley sprigs
few fennel, tarragon or basil sprigs
15ml/1 tbsp black peppercorns
135ml/9 tbsp extra virgin olive oil
plain flour, for coating
salt and ground black pepper
fresh herbs, to garnish

SERVES 4

1 Gut the fish, leaving the head on. Rinse thoroughly inside and out under cold running water. Pat dry with kitchen paper. Spread out half the herbs and peppercorns in the bottom of a large shallow platter, and lay the fish on top. Arrange the remaining herbs over the fish and in its cavity. Sprinkle with 45ml/3 tbsp of the oil. Cover lightly with foil, and chill for 2 hours.

2 Preheat the oven to 200°C/400°F/Gas 6. Remove and discard all the herbs from around the fish. Pat it dry with kitchen paper. Spread a little flour on a large plate and season the fish with salt and pepper. Using a spatula, turn the fish in the flour, shaking off the excess.

3 Heat the remaining olive oil in a flameproof dish just large enough to hold the fish comfortably. When the oil is hot, brown the fish quickly on both sides. Transfer the dish to the oven and bake for 25–40 minutes, depending on the size of the fish. The fish is cooked when the dorsal fin (in the middle of the backbone) comes out easily when pulled. Garnish with the fresh herbs and serve at once.

STUFFED SQUID

Calamari Ripieni

quid are popular all along the coast of the Ligurian sea. They are very tender and easy to cook.

INGREDIENTS
16 medium fresh squid, about 900g/2lb
juice of ½ lemon
2 drained canned anchovy fillets,
chopped
2 garlic cloves, finely chopped
3 tomatoes, peeled, seeded and
finely chopped
30ml/2 tbsp chopped fresh parsley
50g/2oz/1 cup fresh white breadcrumbs
1 egg
30ml/2 tbsp extra virgin olive oil
120ml/4fl oz/½ cup dry white wine
salt and ground black pepper
fresh parsley sprigs, to garnish

SERVES 4

1 Working near the sink, clean each squid in turn by first peeling off the thin skin from the body section. Rinse well. Pull the head and tentacles away from the body sac. Some of the intestines will come away with the head. Remove and discard the translucent quill and any remaining insides from the sac. Sever the tentacles from the head. Discard the head and intestines.

2 Remove and discard the small hard beak from the base of the tentacles. Place the tentacles in a bowl of water with the lemon juice. Rinse all the sacs well under cold running water. Drain and pat dry inside and out with kitchen paper.

3 Preheat the oven to 180°C/350°F/Gas 4. Drain the tentacles. Chop them coarsely and place in a mixing bowl. Stir in the anchovies, garlic, tomatoes, parsley and breadcrumbs. Bind with the egg, then season with salt and pepper. Use this mixture to stuff the squid sacs loosely. Close the opening to the sacs with wooden cocktail sticks.

4 Oil a shallow baking dish large enough to lay the squid in a single layer. Arrange the stuffed squid in the dish. Pour over the remaining oil and wine. Bake, uncovered, for 35–45 minutes or until tender, then serve, garnished with parsley.

TUNA AND BEAN SALAD

Tonno e Fagioli

his substantial salad makes a good light meal, and can be assembled very quickly and easily.

INGREDIENTS

2 x 400g/14oz cans cannellini or borlotti beans
2 x 200g/7oz cans tuna in oil, drained
60ml/4 tbsp extra virgin olive oil
30ml/2 tbsp freshly squeezed lemon juice
15ml/1 tbsp chopped fresh parsley
salt and ground black pepper
30ml/2 tbsp chopped spring onions and a sprig of parsley, to garnish

SERVES 4–6

1 Pour the beans into a large strainer and rinse under cold water. Drain well, then tip into a serving dish.

2 Break the tuna into fairly large flakes and arrange over the beans.

3 Make the dressing in a small bowl. Whisk the oil with the lemon juice, season with salt and pepper, then stir in the parsley. Pour over the beans and tuna.

4 Toss lightly, then garnish by sprinkling over the spring onions *(right)*. Add a sprig of parsley and serve at once.

MIXED SEAFOOD SALAD

Insalata di Frutti di Mare

Popular all over Italy, but particularly along the coast of Tuscany, this makes a superb salad. Use seasonal fresh seafood, or a combination of fresh and frozen ingredients.

INGREDIENTS
350g/12oz small squid
1 small onion, quartered
1 bay leaf
200g/7oz raw prawns, in the shell
675g/1¹⁄₂lb fresh mussels
450g/1lb fresh small clams
175ml/6fl oz/³⁄₄ cup dry white wine
1 fennel bulb

FOR THE DRESSING
75ml/5 tbsp extra virgin olive oil
45ml/3 tbsp freshly squeezed lemon juice
1 garlic clove, finely chopped
salt and ground black pepper

SERVES 6–8

1 Prepare the squid (see Cook's Tip), then carefully rinse the sac and tentacles well under cold running water. Drain and set aside. Bring a large saucepan of water to the boil. Add the onion and bay leaf. Drop in the squid and cook for about 10 minutes, or until they are tender. Remove with a slotted spoon, and allow to cool before slicing the sacs into rings about 1cm/¹⁄₂in wide. Cut each tentacle section into two pieces, then set aside.

2 Add the prawns to the pan of boiling water and cook for about 2 minutes, or until they turn pink. Remove with a slotted spoon. Peel and devein.

3 Scrub the mussels and clams well under cold running water. Cut off the "beards" from the mussels. Place the mussels and clams in a large saucepan with the wine. Cover, and steam until all the shells have opened. Drain the clams and mussels, discarding any that remain closed.

4 Remove all the clams from their shells. Place them in a large serving bowl. Remove all but eight of the mussels from their shells, and add them to the clams in the bowl. Leave the remaining mussels on their half shells, and set them aside.

5 Cut the green, feathery part of the fennel away from the bulb. Chop it finely and set aside. Chop the bulb into bite-size pieces and mix the pieces with the squid and prawns in the serving bowl.

6 Make the dressing by whisking the oil, lemon juice, garlic and chopped fennel green in a small bowl. Add salt and pepper to taste. Pour over the salad, and toss well. Decorate with the reserved mussels and serve.

COOK'S TIP
Clean the squid by peeling off the skin. Rinse, then pull the head and tentacles away from the body. Discard the quill and the insides. Sever the tentacles from the head. Discard the head.

BAKED SEAFOOD SPAGHETTI

Spaghetti Cartoccio

I n this dish, each portion is baked and served in an individual packet which is then opened at the table, releasing a delicious aroma. Use non-stick baking paper to make the packets.

INGREDIENTS
450g/1lb fresh mussels
120ml/4fl oz/½ cup dry white wine
60ml/4 tbsp extra virgin olive oil
2 garlic cloves, finely chopped
450g/1lb tomatoes, peeled and
finely chopped, or
400g/14oz can chopped tomatoes
400g/14oz spaghetti or other long pasta
225g/8oz cooked prawns, peeled and
deveined
30ml/2 tbsp chopped fresh parsley
salt and ground black pepper

SERVES 4

1 Scrub the mussels well under cold running water, cutting off the "beards" with a small sharp knife. Place the mussels in a large saucepan. Add the wine, cover the pan and steam the mussels until they open.

2 Using a slotted spoon, transfer the mussels to a dish, discarding any that remain closed. Strain the cooking liquid through kitchen paper into a jug, and reserve until needed. Preheat the oven to 150°C/300°F/Gas 2.

3 Bring a large saucepan of lightly salted water to the boil. Meanwhile, heat the oil and fry the garlic gently for 1–2 minutes in a separate saucepan. Add the tomatoes, and cook over a medium to high heat until they soften. Stir in 175ml/6fl oz/¾ cup of the cooking liquid from the mussels. Lower the heat so that the sauce barely simmers.

4 Cook the spaghetti in the boiling water for about 12 minutes. Drain well and tip into a serving bowl. Add the prawns and parsley to the tomato sauce, season, and mix into the pasta. Stir in the mussels.

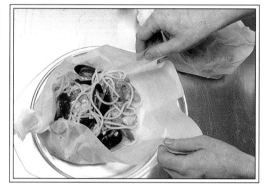

5 Cut four pieces of non-stick baking paper, each measuring about 45 x 30cm/18 x 12in.

6 Place each sheet of paper in a shallow bowl. Divide the pasta mixture among them, mounding it in the centre of each piece of paper, and twisting the ends together to make a closed packet. (The bowls will stop the sauce from spilling while the parcels are being closed.) Arrange the parcels on a large baking sheet, and bake for 8–10 minutes. Place one unopened packet on each serving plate.

COOK'S TIP
Bottled mussels or clams may be substituted for fresh shellfish in this recipe. Add them to the tomato sauce with the prawns.

TUSCAN CHICKEN

Pollo alla Toscana

This simple peasant casserole has all the flavours of traditional Tuscan ingredients. The wine can be replaced by chicken stock, if preferred.

INGREDIENTS
15ml/1 tbsp extra virgin olive oil
8 chicken thighs, skinned
1 onion, thinly sliced
2 red peppers, seeded and sliced
1 garlic clove, crushed
300ml/½ pint/1¼ cups passata (puréed tomatoes)
150ml/¼ pint/⅔ cup dry white wine
1 large oregano sprig, or
5ml/1 tsp dried oregano
400g/14oz can cannellini beans, drained
45ml/3 tbsp fresh white breadcrumbs
salt and ground black pepper
fresh oregano, to garnish

SERVES 4

COOK'S TIP
When herbs are abundant, stir in a handful of fresh oregano leaves just before sprinkling with the breadcrumbs.

---

1 Heat the oil in a heavy-based frying pan which can be used under the grill.

2 Cook the chicken until golden. Remove and keep hot. Add the onion and peppers to the pan and sauté gently until softened. Stir in the garlic. Return the chicken to the pan. Add the tomatoes, wine and oregano, and salt and pepper.

3 Bring to the boil. Cover the pan tightly, lower the heat and simmer for 30–35 minutes or until the chicken is tender.

4 When the chicken is thoroughly cooked, stir in the cannellini beans. Cover the pan again and raise the heat slightly. Leave to simmer for about 5 minutes more, stirring once or twice, until the beans are hot. Preheat the grill.

5 Sprinkle the breadcrumbs evenly over the mixture in the pan and grill until the crumb topping is golden brown. Serve immediately, garnished with fresh oregano.

ROAST CHICKEN WITH FENNEL

Pollo con Finocchio

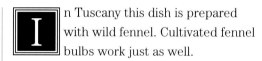n Tuscany this dish is prepared with wild fennel. Cultivated fennel bulbs work just as well.

INGREDIENTS

1.5kg/3–3½ lb roasting chicken
1 onion, quartered
120ml/4fl oz/½ cup extra virgin olive oil
2 fennel bulbs
1 garlic clove, peeled
pinch of grated nutmeg
3–4 thin slices of pancetta or
rindless smoked streaky bacon
120ml/4fl oz/½ cup dry white wine
salt and ground black pepper

SERVES 4–5

1 Preheat the oven to 180°C/350°F/Gas 4. Rinse the chicken in cold water. Pat it dry inside and out with kitchen paper. Sprinkle the cavity with salt and pepper, then place the onion quarters inside. Rub the chicken flesh with about 45ml/3 tbsp of the olive oil. Place in a roasting tin.

2 Cut the feathery green fronds from the tops of the fennel bulbs. Chop the fronds with the garlic. Place in a small bowl and mix with the grated nutmeg. Season with salt and pepper.

3 Sprinkle the fennel mixture over the chicken, pressing it on to the oiled skin. Cover the breast with the slices of pancetta or bacon. Sprinkle with 30ml/2 tbsp of the remaining olive oil. Roast for 30 minutes.

4 Meanwhile, boil or steam the fennel bulbs until barely tender. Remove from the heat and cut lengthways into quarters or sixths. Remove the chicken from the oven and baste it, then arrange the fennel pieces around it. Drizzle the fennel with the remaining oil.

5 Pour about half the wine over the chicken, and return the pan to the oven. Roast the chicken for 30 minutes more, then baste it again. Pour on the remaining wine. Cook for 15–20 minutes more, or until the chicken is cooked through. To test, prick the thigh with a fork. If the juices run clear, the chicken is ready. Transfer it to a serving platter, and arrange the fennel around it. Serve immediately.

PAN-FRIED MARINATED POUSSINS

Galletti Marinati in Padella

hese small birds are full of flavour when marinated for several hours before cooking.

INGREDIENTS

2 poussins, about 450g/1lb each
5–6 mint leaves, torn into pieces
1 leek, sliced into thin rings
1 garlic clove, finely chopped
60ml/4 tbsp extra virgin olive oil
30ml/2 tbsp freshly squeezed lemon juice
50ml/2fl oz/¼ cup dry white wine
salt and ground black pepper
mint leaves, to garnish

SERVES 3–4

1 Cut both poussins in half down the backbone, dividing the breast. Flatten the four halves with a mallet. Place them in a bowl with the mint, leek rings and garlic. Add a generous sprinkling of pepper. Sprinkle with the oil and half the lemon juice, cover, and allow to stand in a cool place for 6 hours.

2 Heat a large heavy-based frying pan. Place the poussins and marinade in the pan, cover, and cook over a medium heat for about 45 minutes. Season with salt. Transfer the poussins to a heated serving platter.

3 Tilt the pan and spoon off any surface fat. Pour in the wine and remaining lemon juice, and cook until the sauce reduces by about half *(right)*. Strain the sauce, pressing the vegetables to extract all the juices. Place the poussin halves on individual heated plates, and spoon over the sauce. Garnish with the mint leaves and serve at once.

QUAIL WITH GRAPES

Quaglie con Uva

Fresh quail are a favourite food in Florence and other Tuscan cities. Use flavourful seedless green grapes for this recipe.

INGREDIENTS
6–8 oven-ready fresh quail
60ml/4 tbsp olive oil
50g/2oz/¼ cup diced pancetta or rindless
smoked streaky bacon
250ml/8fl oz/1 cup dry white wine
250ml/8fl oz/1 cup hot chicken stock
350g/12oz bunch of green grapes
salt and ground black pepper

SERVES 4

1 Wash the quail carefully inside and out with cold water. Pat dry with kitchen paper, then sprinkle salt and pepper into the cavities.

2 Heat the oil in a heavy-based frying pan or casserole large enough to hold all the quail in a single layer. Stir in the pancetta or bacon, and cook over a low heat for 5 minutes.

3 Raise the heat to moderate, and place the quail in the pan. Brown them evenly on all sides. Pour in the wine, and cook over a medium heat until the liquid reduces by about half. Turn the quail over. Cover the pan, and cook for 10–15 minutes more. Add the stock, turn the quail again, cover, and cook for 15–20 minutes, or until the birds are tender. Remove to a warmed serving platter with tongs and keep hot while the sauce is being finished.

4 Bring a saucepan of water to the boil. Drop in the bunch of grapes, and blanch for about 3 minutes. Drain, then pull the grapes from the stem and set aside.

5 Strain the pan juices into a small glass jug. Spoon off any fat from the surface. Pour the strained gravy into a small saucepan. Add the grapes and warm them gently for 2–3 minutes. Spoon around the quail and serve.

ROAST PHEASANT WITH JUNIPER BERRIES

Fagiano Arrosto

S age and juniper are often used in Tuscan cooking to flavour pheasant and other game birds.

INGREDIENTS

1.2–1.4kg/2½–3lb oven-ready pheasant
45ml/3 tbsp olive oil
2 sage sprigs
3 shallots, chopped
1 bay leaf
2 lemon quarters, plus
5ml/1 tsp lemon juice
30ml/2 tbsp juniper berries, crushed
4 thin slices pancetta or streaky bacon
90ml/6 tbsp dry white wine
250ml/8fl oz/1 cup hot chicken stock
25g/1oz/2 tbsp butter, at
room temperature
30ml/2 tbsp plain flour
30ml/2 tbsp brandy
salt and ground black pepper

SERVES 3–4

1 Rub the pheasant with 15ml/1 tbsp of the olive oil. Place the remaining oil, sage leaves, shallots and bay leaf in a shallow bowl. Stir in the lemon juice and juniper berries. Add the pheasant and lemon quarters to the bowl and spoon the marinade over.

2 Cover the dish and allow to stand for several hours in a cool place, turning the pheasant occasionally.

3 Preheat the oven to 180°C/350°F/Gas 4. Place the pheasant in a roasting tin, reserving the marinade. Sprinkle the cavity with salt and pepper. Remove the lemon quarters and bay leaf from the marinade and tuck them inside the bird. Arrange some of the sage leaves from the marinade on the pheasant breast, and lay the pancetta or bacon over the top. Secure with string. Spoon the rest of the marinade and the wine over the pheasant.

4 Roast for about 30 minutes per 450g/1lb, until tender. Baste frequently with the pan juices. Transfer to a serving platter and discard the string and pancetta or bacon.

5 Tilt the roasting tin and skim off any surface fat. Add the stock. Stir over a medium heat, scraping up any residues, then bring to the boil and cook for a few minutes. Strain into a saucepan. Mix the butter to a paste with the flour. Stir into the gravy, a little at a time, then boil for 2–3 minutes, stirring constantly. Remove from the heat, stir in the brandy, and serve in a gravy boat with the pheasant.

DUCK WITH CHESTNUT SAUCE
Petti di Anatra con Salsa di Castagne

This autumnal dish makes use of the sweet chestnuts that are gathered in Italian woods.

INGREDIENTS
1 rosemary sprig
1 garlic clove, thinly sliced
30ml/2 tbsp extra virgin olive oil
4 duck breasts, boned and trimmed
rosemary sprigs, to garnish

FOR THE SAUCE
450g/1lb chestnuts
5ml/1 tsp extra virgin olive oil
350ml/12fl oz/1½ cups milk
1 small onion, finely chopped
1 carrot, finely chopped
1 small bay leaf
30ml/2 tbsp single cream

SERVES 4–5

1 Strip the leaves from the rosemary sprig. Mix them with the garlic and oil in a shallow bowl. Pat the duck breasts dry with kitchen paper. Brush the duck breasts with the marinade and allow to stand for at least 2 hours before cooking.

2 Preheat the oven to 180°C/350°F/Gas 4. Make the sauce. Cut a cross in the flat side of each chestnut with a sharp knife. Place them in a roasting tin with the oil, shaking the pan to coat the nuts thoroughly. Bake for about 20 minutes, then peel.

3 Tip the peeled chestnuts into a heavy-based saucepan and add the milk, onion, carrot and bay leaf. Cook over a low heat for 10–15 minutes until the chestnuts are very tender.

4 Preheat the grill, or prepare a barbecue. Press the chestnut mixture through a sieve into a clean pan. Stir in the cream. Place over a low heat, stirring occasionally.

5 Grill the duck breasts for 6–8 minutes, turning once, until medium rare. The meat should be pink when sliced.

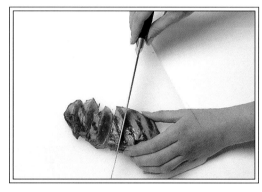

6 Slice the duck into rounds and fan out on heated plates. Garnish with rosemary sprigs and add a portion of chestnut sauce to each plate.

COOK'S TIP
The chestnut sauce can be prepared in advance and kept in the fridge for up to two days, or made when chestnuts are in season and frozen without the cream. Thaw to room temperature before reheating, adding enough single cream to give the consistency of puréed potatoes.

LAMB STEWED WITH TOMATOES AND GARLIC

Spezzatino d'Agnello

T ake a train ride through the Tuscan countryside and you will often see sheep grazing alongside vineyards. This gloriously rustic stew celebrates both farming traditions.

INGREDIENTS
2 large garlic cloves
1 rosemary sprig or 45ml/3 tbsp chopped fresh parsley
60ml/4 tbsp extra virgin olive oil
1.2kg/2½ lb stewing lamb, trimmed and cut into chunks
plain flour seasoned with ground black pepper, for dredging
175ml/6fl oz/¾ cup dry white wine
10ml/2 tsp salt
450g/1lb fresh tomatoes, chopped, or 400g/14oz can chopped tomatoes
120ml/4fl oz/½ cup hot lamb stock

SERVES 5–6

1 Preheat the oven to 180°C/350°F/Gas 4. Chop the garlic with the rosemary leaves or parsley. Heat the oil in a wide flameproof casserole.

2 Add the garlic with the rosemary or parsley, and cook over a medium heat, until the garlic is golden.

3 Toss the lamb in the seasoned flour. Add the lamb to the casserole and cook over a high heat until brown. Remove to a side plate, then pour the wine into the casserole.

4 Bring to the boil, scraping up any meat residues from the bottom. Return the lamb to the casserole and add the salt. Stir in the tomatoes and the stock. Cover the casserole, and bake for 1–2 hours.

BEEF STEW WITH RED WINE

Spezzatino di Manzo

Serve this rich, hearty stew with mashed potatoes or pappardelle noodles.

INGREDIENTS

75ml/5 tbsp extra virgin olive oil
1.2kg/2½lb stewing beef, cut into
4cm/1½in cubes
1 onion, very finely sliced
2 carrots, chopped
45ml/3 tbsp finely chopped fresh parsley
1 garlic clove, chopped
2 bay leaves
few thyme sprigs, or
pinch of dried thyme
pinch of grated nutmeg
250ml/8fl oz/1 cup red wine
400g/14oz can chopped tomatoes
120ml/4fl oz/½ cup beef or chicken stock
15 black olives, stoned and halved
1 large red pepper, seeded and
cut into strips
salt and ground black pepper

SERVES 6

1 Preheat the oven to 180°C/350°F/Gas 4. Heat 45ml/3 tbsp of the oil in a large, heavy-based flameproof casserole. Brown the beef cubes, a few at a time, until coloured on all sides. Using a slotted spoon, transfer each successive batch to a plate.

2 Add the rest of the oil to the fat remaining in the casserole. When it is hot, cook the onion and carrots over a low heat for about 5 minutes or until the onion softens. Add the parsley and garlic and cook for 3–4 minutes more.

3 Return the meat to the pan, raise the heat, and stir well. Stir in the bay leaves, thyme and nutmeg. Add the wine, bring to the boil and cook, stirring, for 4–5 minutes. Stir in the tomatoes, stock and olives, mixing well. Season with salt and pepper. Cover the casserole and bake for 1½ hours.

4 Remove the casserole from the oven. Stir in the pepper strips. Return the casserole to the oven and cook, uncovered, for 30 minutes more, or until the beef is just tender, then serve.

TUSCAN BAKED BEANS

Fagioli al Forno alla Toscana

Both dried and fresh beans are popular in Tuscany, where they are cooked in many different ways. In this simple vegetarian dish they are flavoured with sage leaves.

INGREDIENTS

600g/1lb 6oz/2¾ cups dried beans, such as cannellini
60ml/4 tbsp olive oil
2–3 garlic cloves, crushed
3 sage leaves, torn, or 60ml/4 tbsp chopped fresh parsley
1 leek, finely sliced
400g/14oz can chopped tomatoes
salt and ground black pepper

SERVES 6–8

1 Pick over the beans carefully, discarding any stones or other grit. Place them in a large bowl and add cold water to cover. Soak for at least 6 hours, or overnight, then drain thoroughly.

2 Preheat the oven to 180°C/350°F/Gas 4. Heat the oil in a small saucepan. Add the garlic cloves and sage leaves or parsley and sauté for 3–4 minutes. Remove the pan from the heat.

3 Tip the beans into a large deep baking dish. Add the garlic mixture, then stir in the leek and tomatoes. Pour in enough fresh water to cover the beans by 2.5cm/1in. Mix well. Cover the dish with a lid or foil, and bake for 1¾ hours.

4 Remove the dish from the oven, stir the beans, and season with salt and pepper. Return the beans to the oven, uncovered, and cook for another 15 minutes, or until the beans are tender. Remove from the oven and allow to stand for 7–8 minutes before serving. Serve hot or at room temperature.

STEWED LENTILS

Lenticchie in Umido

I n Tuscany lentils are often eaten as an accompaniment to duck, but they are also good by themselves.

INGREDIENTS

450g/1lb/2 cups green or brown lentils
30ml/2 tbsp extra virgin olive oil
50g/2oz/¼ cup of pancetta, cut into
5cm/2in squares or diced salt pork
1 onion, very finely chopped
1 celery stick, very finely sliced
1 carrot, very finely chopped
1 garlic clove, peeled and left whole
1 bay leaf
45ml/3 tbsp chopped fresh parsley
salt and ground black pepper

SERVES 6

1 Pick over the lentils carefully, removing any stones or other particles. Place them in a large bowl and add water to cover. Soak for several hours, then drain.

2 Heat the oil in a large heavy-based saucepan. Add the pancetta or salt pork and cook for 3–4 minutes. Stir in the onion; cook over a low heat for about 5 minutes.

3 Add the celery and carrot and cook for 3–4 minutes more, stirring occasionally.

4 Tip the lentils into the pan, stirring to coat them with the fat. Pour in enough boiling water just to cover the lentils. Add the whole garlic clove, the bay leaf and the parsley, with salt and pepper to taste. Stir well. Cook over a medium heat for about 1 hour, or until the lentils are tender. Discard the garlic and bay leaf. Serve hot or at room temperature, as you prefer.

BROAD BEAN PURÉE WITH HAM

Purea di Fave con Prosciutto

Peeled broad beans are tender and sweet. They contrast beautifully with slightly salty *prosciutto crudo* in this Tuscan combination.

INGREDIENTS
1kg/2¼lb fresh broad beans in their pods,
or 400g/14oz shelled broad beans, thawed
if frozen
1 onion, finely chopped
2 small potatoes, peeled and diced
45ml/3 tbsp extra virgin olive oil
50g/2oz/¼ cup diced prosciutto crudo
ground black pepper

SERVES 4

1 Place the shelled beans in a saucepan with water to cover. Bring to the boil and cook for 5 minutes. Drain. As soon as they are cool enough to handle, squeeze the beans between finger and thumb to pop them out of their skins.

2 Place the peeled beans in a saucepan and add the onion and potatoes. Pour in enough water just to cover the vegetables. Bring to the boil. Lower the heat slightly, cover and simmer for 15–20 minutes, until the vegetables are very soft. Check the water level occasionally.

3 Heat the oil in a small frying pan and sauté the ham until it is just golden.

4 Purée the bean mixture in a food processor, or mash it by hand. Return it to the pan. If it is too moist, cook it over a medium heat until it reduces slightly. Stir in the ham, with the oil used for cooking it (*right*). Add pepper to taste. Cook for 2 minutes and serve.

Baked Fennel with Pecorino Cheese

Finocchio Gratinato

Fennel is widely eaten in Italy, both raw and cooked. It is delicious with pecorino or Parmesan cheese in this quick and simple dish.

INGREDIENTS
1kg/2¼lb fennel bulbs, washed and cut in half
50g/2oz/4 tbsp butter
40g/1½oz/½ cup freshly grated pecorino or Parmesan cheese

SERVES 4–6

1 Bring a large saucepan of water to the boil, add the fennel and cook for about 10 minutes until tender, then drain.

2 Preheat the oven to 200°C/400°F/Gas 6. Cut the fennel lengthways into four or six pieces. Place in a buttered baking dish.

3 Dot the fennel with the butter and sprinkle with the grated cheese. Bake for about 20 minutes, or until the cheese is golden brown. Serve immediately.

VARIATION
For a more substantial version of this dish, sprinkle 75g/3oz/½ cup chopped ham over the fennel before topping with the cheese.

BROCCOLI WITH OIL AND GARLIC
Broccoletti Saltati con Olio e Aglio

This is a very simple way of transforming steamed or blanched broccoli into a succulent Mediterranean dish. Peeling the broccoli stalks is easy, and allows for even cooking.

INGREDIENTS
1kg/2¼lb fresh broccoli
90ml/6 tbsp extra virgin olive oil
2–3 garlic cloves, finely chopped
salt and ground black pepper

SERVES 6

1 Wash the broccoli. Using a small sharp knife, cut off any woody parts at the base of the broccoli, then peel the stems. Cut any very long or wide stalks in half.

2 Boil some water in the bottom of a saucepan equipped with a steamer, or bring a large saucepan of water to the boil. If steaming the broccoli, put it in the steamer and cover tightly. Cook for 8–12 minutes or until the stems are just tender when pierced with the point of a knife. Remove from the heat. If blanching, drop the broccoli into the pan of boiling water and cook for 5–6 minutes, until just tender.

3 In a frying pan large enough to hold all the broccoli pieces, gently heat the oil with the garlic. When the garlic is light golden (do not let it brown or it will be bitter) add the broccoli, and cook over moderate heat for 3–4 minutes, turning carefully to coat it with the hot oil. Tip into a serving bowl and season with salt and pepper. Serve hot or cold.

SAUTÉED PEAS WITH HAM
Piselli alla Fiorentina

When fresh peas are in season in Florence, they are stewed with a little ham and onion and served as a substantial side dish.

INGREDIENTS
45ml/3 tbsp extra virgin olive oil
115g/4oz/1/2 cup diced pancetta or
rindless smoked streaky bacon
45ml/3 tbsp finely chopped onion
1kg/2¼lb peas in the pod (about
300g/11oz shelled) or 275g/10oz frozen
petits pois, thawed
30–45ml/2–3 tbsp water
few mint leaves or parsley sprigs
salt and ground black pepper

SERVES 4

1 Heat the oil in a medium saucepan, and sauté the pancetta or bacon and onion for 2–3 minutes.

2 Stir in the shelled fresh or thawed frozen peas. Add the water. Season with salt and pepper and mix well to coat with the oil.

3 Add the fresh herbs, cover, and cook over a medium heat until tender. This may take from 5 minutes for sweet fresh peas, to 15 for tougher, older peas. Serve as a side dish with meat or omelette dishes.

GRILLED RADICCHIO AND COURGETTES

Verdure ai Ferri

Tuscan cooks relish the flavour of radicchio, grilled or barbecued. It is delicious and very quick and easy to prepare.

INGREDIENTS
2–3 firm heads of radicchio
4 courgettes
90ml/6 tbsp extra virgin olive oil
salt and ground black pepper

SERVES 4

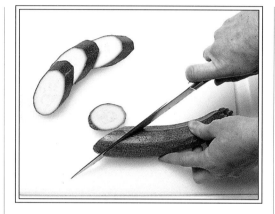

2 Using a sharp knife, cut the courgettes into 1cm/½in diagonal slices.

1 Preheat the grill, or prepare a barbecue. Cut the radicchio in half through the root section or base. If necessary, wash in cold water, then drain.

3 When the grill is hot or the barbecue is ready, brush the vegetables all over with the oil, and sprinkle them with salt and pepper. Cook on a rack for 4–5 minutes on each side. Serve as a starter or as an accompaniment to grilled fish or meat.

PIZZA WITH HERBS

Pizza in Bianco con Erbe Aromatiche

his simple topping of fresh herbs, olive oil and salt makes a pizza bread that is delicious served hot.

INGREDIENTS
275g/10oz/2½ cups plain flour
2.5ml/½ tsp salt
5ml/1 tsp easy-blend dried yeast
175ml/6fl oz/¾ cup warm water
30ml/2 tbsp olive oil

FOR THE TOPPING
60ml/4 tbsp chopped mixed fresh herbs
coarse sea salt, to taste
90ml/6 tbsp extra virgin olive oil

SERVES 4

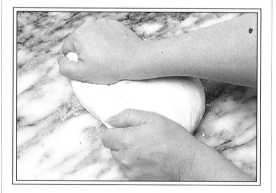

1 Sift the flour, salt and yeast into a bowl. Add the water and oil and mix to a soft dough. Knead for 5 minutes until smooth.

2 Lightly flour the work surface and then roll out the dough to a 25cm/10in round, making the edges of the round slightly thicker than the centre.

3 Transfer the round to a lightly oiled pizza tin or baking sheet, then pinch up the edges to form a shallow rim.

4 Sprinkle over the herbs and salt, and drizzle with the olive oil. Leave to rise in a warm place for 30 minutes. Preheat the oven to 240°C/475°F/Gas 9. Bake for 25–30 minutes, until golden. Serve immediately.

ITALIAN BREAD STICKS

Grissini

These typically Italian bread sticks are especially delicious when hand-made. They are still sold loose in many bakeries in Turin and northern Italy.

INGREDIENTS
15g/½oz/1½ tbsp fresh cake yeast or
7g/¼oz/½ tbsp active dried yeast
120ml/4fl oz/½ cup lukewarm water
pinch of sugar
5ml/1 tsp salt
200–225g/7–8oz/1¾ cups plain flour

MAKES ABOUT 30

1 Warm a mixing bowl by swirling some hot water in it, then drain. Put the yeast in the bowl, and pour on the warm water. Mix in the sugar, and allow to stand for about 10 minutes until the yeast starts to foam. Using a wooden spoon, mix in the salt and one-third of the flour. Mix in another third of the flour, stirring, until the dough forms a mass and pulls away from the sides of the bowl.

2 Sprinkle some of the remaining flour on to a work surface. Remove all the dough from the bowl and knead for 8–10 minutes, until the dough is smooth.

3 Tear a lump, the size of a small walnut, from the ball of dough. Roll it lightly between your hands into a small sausage shape. Set it aside on a lightly floured surface. Repeat until all the dough is used up and there are about 30 pieces.

4 Place one piece of dough at a time on a clean work surface without any flour on it. With both hands and your fingers spread, roll each piece of dough backwards and forwards into a long strand about 1cm/½in thick. Transfer to a lightly greased baking tray.

5 Preheat the oven to 200°C/400°F/Gas 6. Cover the tray with a cloth and leave the grissini in a warm place to rise for about 15 minutes while the oven is heating up.

6 Bake for 8–10 minutes, then remove from the oven. Turn the grissini over and put them back in the oven for 6–7 minutes more. Do not let them brown. Remove from the oven and allow to cool before serving. The grissini should be crisp when served. If they lose their crispness on a damp day, you can warm them in a moderate oven for a few minutes just before serving.

FOCACCIA

Focaccia

F ocaccia is a form of flat bread that is oiled before baking. It is usually made in a large baking tray, and sold in bakeries cut into squares.

INGREDIENTS
275g/10oz/2½ cups plain flour
2.5ml/½ tsp salt
5ml/1 tsp easy-blend dried yeast
175ml/6fl oz/¾ cup warm water
30ml/2 tbsp olive oil
45ml/3 tbsp extra virgin olive oil
coarse sea salt

SERVES 6–8

1 Sift the flour, salt and yeast into a mixing bowl and make a well in the centre. Pour the water and olive oil into the well and mix to a soft dough. Knead for 5–10 minutes until smooth and elastic. Punch the dough down to remove any air.

2 Place the dough in a lightly oiled baking tin, then use your fingers to press it into an even layer 2cm/¾in thick.

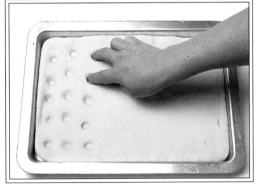

3 Cover the dough with a cloth and leave to rise in a warm place for 30 minutes. In the mean time, preheat the oven to 200°C/400°F/Gas 6. When the dough has risen, make light indents in the bread's surface using your fingers.

4 Brush the dough with the extra virgin oil, sprinkle with the salt and bake for about 25 minutes, or until just golden. Cut into squares or wedges and serve warm or at room temperature, as a side dish to a meal or as a snack on its own.

FOCACCIA WITH OLIVES

Focaccia con Olive

Green olives make a classic topping for this Italian speciality – scatter over tiny fresh rosemary sprigs in place of the olives for a fragrant alternative.

INGREDIENTS
275g/10oz/2½ cups plain flour
2.5ml/½ tsp salt
5ml/1 tsp easy-blend dried yeast
175ml/6fl oz/¾ cup warm water
75ml/5 tbsp olive oil
10–12 large green olives, stoned and cut in half lengthways
coarse sea salt

SERVES 6–8

1 Sift the flour, salt and yeast into a mixing bowl and make a well in the centre. Pour the water and 30ml/2 tbsp of the olive oil into the well and mix to a soft dough. Knead for 5–10 minutes until smooth and elastic. Brush a large round or square shallow baking tin with 15ml/1 tbsp of the remaining oil. Place the dough in the tin, and press it into an even layer 2cm/¾in thick.

2 Cover the dough with a cloth and leave for 30 minutes. Preheat the oven to 200°C/400°F/Gas 6. Make light holes in the bread's surface and brush with the oil.

3 Dot evenly with the olive pieces, and sprinkle with a little coarse salt. Bake for about 25 minutes, or until just golden. Cut into squares or wedges and serve warm or at room temperature, either as a side dish with a meal, or on its own.

BREAD WITH GRAPES

Schiacciata con Uva

his bread is made with wine grapes in central Italy to celebrate the grape harvest there.

INGREDIENTS
750g/1¾lb small black grapes
115g/4oz/½ cup sugar
275g/10oz/2½ cups plain flour
2.5ml/½ tsp salt
5ml/1 tsp easy-blend dried yeast
175ml/6fl oz/¾ cup warm water
30ml/2 tbsp olive oil
30ml/2 tbsp extra virgin olive oil

SERVES 6–8

1 Preheat the oven to 190°C/375°F/Gas 5. Remove the grapes from the stems, wash them and pat dry with kitchen paper. Place in a bowl and sprinkle with the sugar.

2 Sift the flour, salt and yeast into a bowl, make a well in the centre and pour in the water and olive oil. Mix to a soft dough, then knead for 5–10 minutes until smooth.

3 Divide the dough in half. Roll out each piece to a 20cm/8in round. Place one half on a lightly greased baking sheet and sprinkle with the sugared grapes.

4 Top with the second round of dough and crimp the edges together. Sprinkle the remaining grapes over the top. Cover loosely and leave to rise in warm place for about 30 minutes.

5 Drizzle the extra virgin olive oil over the bread and bake for 50–60 minutes. Allow to cool before cutting into wedges, then serve.

PEACHES WITH AMARETTI STUFFING

Pesche con Amaretti

P eaches are plentiful all over Italy. This is one of the most delectable ways of serving them.

INGREDIENTS
4 fresh ripe peaches
juice of ½ lemon
65g/2½oz/1 cup crushed
amaretti biscuits
30ml/2 tbsp Marsala, brandy or
peach brandy
25g/1oz/2 tbsp butter, at room
temperature
2.5ml/½ tsp vanilla essence
30ml/2 tbsp granulated sugar
1 egg yolk

SERVES 4

2 Put the amaretti crumbs in a bowl, add the Marsala or brandy and leave to soften for a few minutes. In a separate bowl, beat the butter. Stir in the amaretti mixture, with the vanilla essence, sugar, and egg yolk.

1 Preheat the oven to 180°C/350°F/Gas 4. Wash and dry the peaches. Cut them in half and remove the stones. Enlarge the hollow left by the stones by scooping out some of each peach. Sprinkle the peach halves with the lemon juice.

3 Arrange the peach halves in a baking dish in a single layer with the hollow sides upwards. Divide the amaretti mixture among the hollows, mounding it in the centre. Bake for 35–40 minutes and serve hot or cold.

CHESTNUT PUDDING

Budino di Castagne

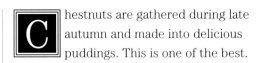

Chestnuts are gathered during late autumn and made into delicious puddings. This is one of the best.

INGREDIENTS
450g/1lb fresh chestnuts
300ml/¹/₂ pint/1¹/₄ cups milk
115g/4oz/¹/₂ cup caster sugar
2 eggs, separated, at room temperature
25g/1oz/¹/₄ cup cocoa powder
2.5ml/¹/₂ tsp vanilla essence
50g/2oz/scant ¹/₂ cup icing sugar, sifted
butter, for greasing
whipped cream and marrons glacés,
to decorate

SERVES 4–5

1 Preheat the oven to 180°C/350°F/Gas 4. Butter four individual pudding bowls. Cut a cross in the flat side of each chestnut. Cook the chestnuts in boiling water for 5–6 minutes. Remove with a slotted spoon, and peel off the skins while still warm.

2 Place the peeled chestnuts in a heavy-based or non-stick saucepan. Add the milk and half the caster sugar. Cook over a low heat, stirring occasionally, until soft. Allow to cool, then press the contents of the pan through a strainer into a clean bowl.

3 In a separate bowl, beat the egg yolks with the remaining caster sugar until the mixture is pale yellow and fluffy. Beat in the cocoa powder and the vanilla. Using a wire whisk or hand-held electric beater, whisk the egg whites until they form soft peaks. Beat in the sifted icing sugar. Continue beating until the mixture forms stiff peaks.

4 Fold the chestnut and egg yolk mixtures together, then the egg whites. Spoon into the greased bowls. Place on a baking sheet and bake for 15–20 minutes. Cool for 10 minutes before turning the puddings out. Pipe with whipped cream and decorate with marrons glacés.

POACHED PEARS IN RED WINE

Pere cotte Rosse

INGREDIENTS
1 bottle red wine
150g/5oz/⅔ cup caster sugar
45ml/3 tbsp clear honey
juice of ½ lemon
1 cinnamon stick
1 vanilla pod, split open lengthways
5cm/2in piece of orange rind
1 clove
1 black peppercorn
4 firm ripe pears of similar size
whipped cream or soured cream, to serve

SERVES 4

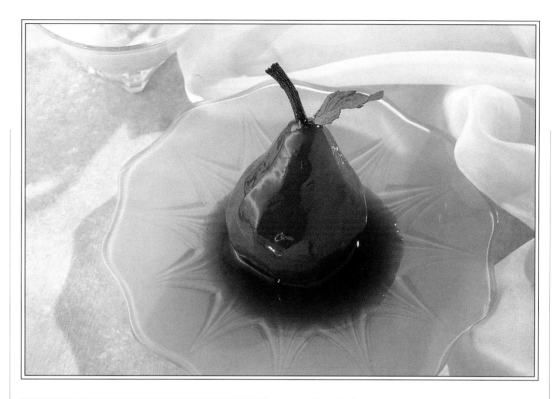

1 Place the red wine, caster sugar, honey, lemon juice, cinnamon stick, vanilla pod, orange rind, clove and peppercorn in a saucepan just large enough to hold the pears upright. Heat gently over a low heat, stirring occasionally, until the sugar has completely dissolved.

2 Meanwhile, peel the pears, leaving the stem on each intact. Take a thin slice off the base of each pear so that it will stand level on a serving dish.

3 Stand the pears upright in the wine mixture. Simmer, uncovered, for 20–35 minutes depending on size and ripeness, until the pears are just tender; be careful not to overcook. Test gently with the tip of a sharp knife.

4 Using a slotted spoon, carefully transfer the pears to a bowl. Continue to boil the poaching liquid until reduced by about half. Leave to cool, then strain the cooled liquid over the pears and chill for at least 3 hours.

5 Place each pear in an individual serving dish and spoon over a little of the red wine syrup. Serve with chilled whipped or soured cream.

INDEX